ARLES

"YOUR ULTIMATE TRAVEL GUIDE"

Halie Boyle

1

AUTHOR EXPERIENCE

My journey through Arles was nothing short of inspiring. The city, steeped in history and bathed in Provençal charm, felt like a step back in time. From the moment I arrived, I was captivated by the ancient Roman architecture, including the iconic Arles Amphitheater and Roman Theater. Walking through these monumental sites, I could almost hear the echoes of gladiatorial battles and theatrical performances from centuries past. The preservation of these ruins and the stories they tell made Arles feel like an open-air museum, offering history enthusiasts endless discoveries.

What struck me most was the artistic spirit of Arles, deeply tied to Vincent van Gogh's legacy. As I traced his footsteps through the Van Gogh Trail and visited the Fondation Vincent van Gogh, I felt a profound connection to the painter's life and work. Standing at the very spot where he painted Café Terrace at Night was a surreal experience, made even more vivid by the golden glow of the evening lights. The city seemed to embody his artistic vision, with its vibrant colors, textured landscapes, and serene Rhône River providing endless inspiration for any traveler with an appreciation for art.

Exploring the Camargue region was another highlight of my visit. Just a short drive from Arles, this natural haven introduced me to its wild horses, pink flamingos, and vast salt marshes. Riding horseback through the picturesque landscapes was an unforgettable adventure, allowing me to connect with the unique beauty of Provence beyond the city. The trip to the Camargue reminded me of the diversity Arles offers not only as a historic and cultural hub but also as a gateway to extraordinary natural wonders.

Finally, my experience of Provençal culture through the food, markets, and people of Arles left a lasting impression. The bustling Saturday market was a feast for the senses, brimming with fresh produce, local delicacies, and artisanal crafts. Dining at local restaurants gave me a true taste of Provençal cuisine, from fragrant ratatouille to freshly baked fougasse. The warm hospitality of the locals made my stay even more memorable, reminding me that travel is not just about places, but also the people you meet along the way.

TABLE OF CONTENTS

CHAPTER 1

Introduction to Arles

Arles, a historic city in southern France, is renowned for its rich cultural heritage, stunning Roman monuments, and deep connection to art and history. Situated along the Rhône River in the Provence-Alpes-Côte d'Azur région, it was once a thriving Roman settlement often called "The Little Rome of Gaul." Today, Arles is a UNESCO World Heritage Site, celebrated for its well-preserved Roman amphitheater, ancient theater, and thermal baths. The city's narrow streets, vibrant squares, and Provençal charm captivate visitors, while its role in inspiring artists like Vincent van Gogh has cemented its place in the cultural landscape.

Arles is a gateway to the natural wonders of the Camargue region, known for its wild horses, pink flamingos, and serene wetlands. Its bustling markets, annual festivals, and strong ties to both Roman and Provençal traditions make it a dynamic destination year-round. Arles is more than just a city; it is a living testament to the seamless integration of history, art, and natural beauty, offering visitors an unforgettable experience.

Overview of Arles

Arles, a charming city in the Provence-Alpes-Côte d'Azur region of southern France, is celebrated for its remarkable blend of history, art, and culture. Nestled on the banks of the Rhône River, it is a city with roots that stretch back over 2,500 years, earning its place as a UNESCO World Heritage Site. Arles was a significant Roman settlement, often referred to as "The Little Rome of Gaul," and its well-preserved Roman amphitheater, theater, and baths remain some of the most iconic landmarks of its illustrious past. The city's cobblestone streets, sunlit squares, and colorful architecture reflect its Provençal charm, while its vibrant cultural scene continues to captivate locals and visitors alike.

Beyond its historical significance, Arles is famous for its deep connection to the arts, particularly through Vincent van Gogh, who painted some of his most famous works during his time in the city. Today, Arles hosts numerous cultural events, such as the Rencontres d'Arles photography festival, which draws international attention. The nearby Camargue Natural Park adds another layer of allure, offering breathtaking landscapes filled with wild horses, flamingos, and salt flats. Whether exploring its Roman heritage, strolling through the Van Gogh trail, or immersing oneself in Provençal culture, Arles offers a multifaceted experience that leaves a lasting impression.

Historical Significance of the City

Arles has a history that stretches back over 2,500 years, beginning as a settlement for the Ligurians before becoming a thriving Roman colony in 46 BC under Julius Caesar. During the Roman period, it was a cultural and economic powerhouse, often referred to as

"The Little Rome of Gaul." Its Roman architecture, including the amphitheater, theater, and aqueducts, reflects its importance as a provincial capital in ancient times.

In the early Christian period, Arles played a pivotal role as a center of religious activity, hosting the Council of Arles in 314 AD, which shaped early Christian theology. During the Middle Ages, Arles was an influential trading hub and maintained its prominence due to its location along the Rhône River. Its significance in the arts and culture continued to evolve, particularly during the 19th century, when Vincent van Gogh painted over 300 works inspired by the city's light, landscapes, and people.

The city's historical significance is preserved in its well-maintained monuments and sites, making it a treasure trove for history enthusiasts and scholars alike.

Key Highlights of Arles

Arles boasts an impressive array of attractions that captivate visitors with their beauty and historical value. Among the city's most notable highlights are:

Roman Monuments
Arles Amphitheater: A two-tiered structure built in the 1st century AD, this amphitheater was used for gladiator battles and can still host events today.

Roman Theater: An ancient performance venue that once accommodated 8,000 spectators and now serves as a site for cultural events and concerts.

Thermae of Constantine: These Roman baths offer insight into the luxurious lifestyles of the ancient elite.

Artistic and Cultural Legacy
Van Gogh Trail: Walk in the footsteps of Vincent van Gogh, who immortalized Arles in some of his most famous paintings, such as Starry Night Over the Rhône and Café Terrace at Night.
Fondation Vincent van Gogh: A museum dedicated to the artist's works and influence on Arles.

Rencontres d'Arles: An annual international photography festival that attracts photographers and enthusiasts worldwide.

Religious Sites
St. Trophime Church: A masterpiece of Romanesque architecture featuring intricate carvings and a cloister that exudes serenity.

Alyscamps: A Roman necropolis that was later repurposed as a Christian burial ground and inspired van Gogh and Paul Gauguin.

Nature and Landscape
Camargue Natural Park: Located just outside Arles, this vast wetland is known for its unique biodiversity, including wild horses, pink flamingos, and salt flats.

Best Times to Visit

Arles is a year-round destination, but the best time to visit depends on your preferences for weather and activities.

Spring (March to May)
Spring offers mild temperatures and vibrant landscapes, making it the ideal time for outdoor exploration and visiting the Camargue Natural Park. The city is less crowded, and festivals like Feria de Pâques (Easter Festival) showcase Arles' bullfighting traditions and culture.

Summer (June to August)
Summer is the peak tourist season, with long days and warm weather. The Rencontres d'Arles photography festival takes place during this time, adding an artistic vibrancy to the city. However, the heat can be intense, so visitors should plan outdoor activities in the early morning or evening.

Autumn (September to November)
The autumn months bring cooler weather and fewer tourists, offering a more relaxed experience. This season is perfect for exploring the city's historical sites and enjoying the golden hues of the surrounding countryside.

Winter (December to February)
While quieter in winter, Arles retains its charm with a festive atmosphere during the Christmas season. The

city's markets and cultural events continue, and the mild climate makes it comfortable for sightseeing.

Arles is a city where every season brings its unique charm, ensuring an unforgettable experience regardless of when you choose to visit.

CHAPTER 2

Getting to Arles

Arles is well-connected and accessible via various transportation modes, making it an easy destination for travelers from France and beyond. By train, visitors can reach Arles through the French national rail network (SNCF). High-speed TGV trains connect nearby hubs such as Avignon and Marseille to major cities like Paris, while regional TER trains provide direct access to Arles. For those traveling by air, the closest airports include Marseille Provence Airport (about 70 km away), Nîmes Airport (25 km away), and Montpellier Airport (75 km away). From these airports, travelers can use shuttle buses, trains, or rental cars to reach Arles.

Driving to Arles is another convenient option, especially for those exploring Provence. The city is connected by major highways, including the A54 and N570, offering easy routes from nearby cities like Marseille, Avignon, and Montpellier. Parking options are available on the outskirts of the city center, as the historic district is best explored on foot. For budget-conscious travelers, intercity buses operated by regional providers like LER and Cartreize are an economical way to reach Arles from nearby towns and cities. With its diverse transport options, getting to Arles is both straightforward and flexible for all types of travelers.

Transportation Options

Arles can be reached through multiple transportation options, ensuring flexibility for visitors traveling from within France or abroad.

By Train
France's efficient train network makes reaching Arles simple and convenient. The city is part of the national SNCF train network, and direct trains connect it to major French cities such as Paris, Marseille, Lyon, and Avignon. High-speed trains (TGV) to nearby hubs like Avignon and Marseille allow travelers to continue their journey to Arles with regional TER trains. The scenic train ride through Provence enhances the travel experience.

By Air
Although Arles does not have its own airport, it is within a short distance of several major airports, offering domestic and international flights. From the airports, travelers can use trains, buses, or rental cars to reach the city.

By Car
Driving to Arles is an excellent choice for those who wish to explore the surrounding region. With well-maintained roads and highways, the city is easily accessible by car from other parts of France and neighboring countries. Car rentals are widely available for those flying into regional airports.

By Bus

Regional and intercity buses connect Arles to nearby towns and cities. These are an economical option, especially for travelers arriving from smaller towns in Provence or the Camargue region. Bus services are operated by regional providers such as LER and Cartreize, offering a reliable and cost-effective alternative to trains.

Nearest Airports and Train Stations

Airports Near Arles

Arles is conveniently located near several airports, making air travel a practical option. The three nearest airports are:

Marseille Provence Airport (MRS)

Distance: Approximately 70 kilometers (43 miles)

Travel Time: Around 1 hour by car or train

Features: Marseille Provence Airport is the largest and most convenient airport for reaching Arles, with numerous international and domestic flights.

Nîmes–Alès–Camargue–Cévennes Airport (FNI)**

Distance: Approximately 25 kilometers (15 miles)

Travel Time: Around 30 minutes by car

Features: A smaller airport with limited flights, primarily serving low-cost airlines and regional destinations.

Montpellier-Méditerranée Airport (MPL)**

Distance: Approximately 75 kilometers (47 miles)

Travel Time: Around 1 hour by car

Features: An international airport offering flights to several European destinations.

Train Stations Near Arles

Arles is served by its own train station, ensuring seamless access by rail:

Arles Train Station (Gare d'Arles)

Location: Close to the city center, within walking distance of major attractions.

Features: Serves regional TER trains connecting Arles to Avignon, Marseille, Nîmes, and beyond.

Accessibility: A small but well-organized station with ticket counters, vending machines, and taxi services.

Nearby High-Speed Rail (TGV) Stations

Avignon TGV Station: Located about 40 kilometers (25 miles) from Arles, this station offers high-speed connections to Paris, Lyon, and other major cities.

Nîmes Pont du Gard Station: Another TGV station close to Arles, providing fast links to northern France and beyond.

Travelers arriving at high-speed rail hubs can easily transfer to regional trains or buses to reach Arles.

Driving to Arles: Tips and Routes

Major Routes to Arles
Arles is well-connected by road, with several major highways and scenic routes leading to the city.

From Marseille
Distance: Approximately 90 kilometers (56 miles)
Route: Follow the A7 highway, then connect to the A54 towards Arles.
Estimated Travel Time: 1 hour.

From Avignon
Distance: Approximately 40 kilometers (25 miles)
Route: Take the N570 road directly to Arles.
Estimated Travel Time: 40 minutes.

From Montpellier
Distance: Approximately 75 kilometers (47 miles)
Route: Take the A9 highway, then connect to the A54.
Estimated Travel Time: 1 hour.

From Paris
Distance: Approximately 730 kilometers (453 miles)

Route: Use the A6 highway to Lyon, then follow the A7 to the south and A54 to Arles.

Estimated Travel Time: 7 hours.

Driving Tips
Parking in Arles: The city center has limited parking, so it's best to use designated parking lots on the outskirts and walk to the historic district.

Parking des Lices and Parking Lamartine.
Tolls: French highways often have tolls, so carry cash or a credit card for payment.

Scenic Routes: Consider taking the slower D roads to enjoy the stunning landscapes of Provence.

Navigation: Use GPS or a detailed map to plan your route, as some city streets can be narrow and tricky to navigate.

Local Transport Within the City

Once in Arles, getting around is straightforward, thanks to its compact size and pedestrian-friendly layout.

Walking
Arles' historic center is best explored on foot. Most major attractions, including the Roman amphitheater, Van Gogh sites, and museums, are within walking distance of each other. The city's narrow streets, picturesque alleys, and charming squares make walking an enjoyable way to soak in its ambiance.

Bicycles

Cycling is a popular and eco-friendly way to navigate Arles and its surroundings. Several bike rental shops are available in the city, and dedicated cycling paths extend to nearby areas, including the Camargue. The flat terrain makes it easy for all levels of cyclists.

Public Buses

Arles has a small but reliable bus network operated by Envia, which connects key areas within the city and nearby villages. Tickets are affordable, and buses run regularly, making it a practical option for those who prefer not to walk.

Taxis and Ridesharing

Taxis are available at the train station and other central locations, though they can be more expensive than public transport.

Car Rentals

For those wishing to explore beyond the city limits, renting a car is a good option. Rental agencies are located near the train station and at nearby airports. A car provides the flexibility to visit attractions like the Camargue Natural Park or nearby Provençal villages at your own pace.

Tourist Trains

Arles also offers a small tourist train that provides a guided tour of the main landmarks. This is an excellent option for families or visitors with limited mobility who want a quick overview of the city.

CHAPTER 3

Exploring Arles' Roman Heritage

Arles, often referred to as "The Little Rome of Gaul," is home to some of the most remarkable Roman monuments in Europe, offering a vivid glimpse into the grandeur of ancient civilization. Its Roman heritage is showcased through iconic sites such as the Roman Amphitheatre (Arènes d'Arles), the Ancient Theatre, the Alyscamps Necropolis, and the Roman Baths of Constantine. These structures highlight the architectural brilliance and cultural significance of the Roman Empire. From gladiatorial games and theatrical performances to sacred burial practices and communal baths, Arles' Roman sites provide insight into the social, cultural, and spiritual life of antiquity.

Each monument tells a unique story of transformation and preservation. The Roman Amphitheatre, once a venue for thrilling spectacles, continues to host events today, while the Ancient Theatre, originally a hub for artistic expression, now serves as a cultural stage for modern performances. The Alyscamps Necropolis, with its storied sarcophagi and links to early Christianity, exudes an aura of sacred history, immortalized by artists like Van Gogh. Meanwhile, the Roman Baths of Constantine showcase the Romans' advanced engineering and communal traditions. Together, these landmarks not only connect us to Arles' glorious past but also reinforce the city's status as a global destination for historical and cultural exploration.

The Roman Amphitheatre (Arènes d'Arles)

The Roman Amphitheatre of Arles, commonly referred to as the Arènes d'Arles, was constructed in 90 AD during the reign of Emperor Domitian. Designed to host gladiatorial combats, animal fights, and other spectacles, it could accommodate approximately 20,000 spectators, making it one of the largest amphitheatres in Roman Gaul.

Architecture and Design
The amphitheatre is an elliptical structure, measuring about 136 meters in length and 107 meters in width, with an impressive facade featuring two tiers of 60 arches each. The design mirrors the Colosseum in Rome, showcasing the ingenuity of Roman engineering. Its advanced drainage system and tiered seating ensured smooth operations during events.

Transformation Over Time
After the fall of the Roman Empire, the amphitheatre was repurposed as a fortress during the Middle Ages. Houses and chapels were built within its walls, which transformed it into a small village. It wasn't until the 19th century that efforts were made to restore it to its former glory. Today, it serves as a venue for bullfighting events, concerts, and historical reenactments.

Significance

The amphitheatre remains a symbol of Arles' Roman heritage. It has been recognized as a UNESCO World Heritage Site since 1981, drawing tourists and historians from around the world.

Ancient Theatre of Arles

Construction and Purpose

Built in the late 1st century BC During the reign of Emperor Augustus, the Ancient Theatre of Arles was among the first stone theatres constructed in Gaul. It was primarily used for theatrical performances, poetry recitals, and other cultural activities, demonstrating the Romans' emphasis on arts and entertainment.

Architectural Features

The theatre originally had a seating capacity of 10,000 spectators, arranged in semicircular tiers. At its peak, it featured an elaborate stage backdrop (scaenae frons) adorned with columns, statues, and reliefs. The orchestra pit at the base was reserved for musicians and important officials.

A notable find from the site is the Venus of Arles, a stunning marble statue discovered in the 17th century and now housed in the Louvre Museum.

Decline and Rediscovery

Like the amphitheatre, the theatre fell into disuse after the Roman period and was quarried for stone during the Middle Ages. Archaeological excavations in the 19th century uncovered its remains, leading to its partial restoration.

Cultural Importance
Today, the Ancient Theatre is an active cultural venue, hosting concerts, plays, and the Les Rencontres d'Arles photography festival. It serves as a bridge between ancient Roman culture and contemporary artistic expression.

Alyscamps Necropolis

The Alyscamps, derived from the Latin term Elysii Campi (Elysian Fields), is one of the most famous Roman necropolises. Located just outside the ancient city walls, it became a prominent burial site in Roman times, with rows of stone sarcophagi lining the road leading to the city.

Role in Early Christianity
In the 4th century, the Alyscamps gained significance as a Christian burial site after the martyrdom of Saint Genesius of Arles, whose burial here attracted pilgrims. The necropolis became a holy site, with additional chapels constructed to honor the dead.

Artistic and Historical Value
The Alyscamps is renowned for its collection of elaborate sarcophagi, many of which feature intricate carvings depicting Roman mythology, biblical scenes, and floral motifs. Over time, many of these artifacts were removed

and placed in museums, but the site still retains its spiritual and historical essence.

Decline and Modern Recognition
With the rise of newer cemeteries in the 12th century, the Alyscamps fell into decline. However, its evocative atmosphere and historical depth have inspired numerous artists, including Vincent van Gogh and Paul Gauguin, who immortalized the site in their paintings. Today, the necropolis is a UNESCO-listed site and a popular tourist destination.

The Roman Baths of Constantine

The Roman Baths of Constantine, also known as Thermae Constantini, date back to the 4th century AD and are believed to have been commissioned during the reign of Emperor Constantine I or his successors. Public baths were an integral part of Roman society, serving as centers for hygiene, relaxation, and social interaction.

Architectural Features
Although much of the original complex has been lost, the surviving structures provide insight into Roman bathing culture. The baths featured three main sections:

Caldarium (hot bath)

Tepidarium (warm bath)

Frigidarium (cold bath)

The remnants of the caldarium are particularly impressive, showcasing large arched windows that allowed natural light to flood the interior. The complex also included a palaestra (exercise area) and a courtyard.

Later Use and Rediscovery
After the decline of the Roman Empire, the baths were abandoned and repurposed for other uses during the medieval period. Excavations in the 19th and 20th centuries uncovered the site, shedding light on its historical significance.

Modern-Day Significance
Today, the Roman Baths of Constantine are a preserved archaeological site that offers visitors a glimpse into the sophistication of Roman engineering and the importance of communal spaces in ancient society.

CHAPTER 4

Art and Culture

Arles is a city deeply rooted in art and culture, where its rich history and vibrant creativity intersect. The city is famously associated with Vincent van Gogh, who created over 300 works during his stay, drawing inspiration from the town's serene landscapes and striking light. This connection to Van Gogh, coupled with its world-class museums such as the Musée Réattu and the Musée de l'Arles Antique, highlights Arles' status as a haven for art lovers. These institutions preserve the city's Roman heritage, showcase contemporary art, and celebrate regional traditions, making Arles a multifaceted cultural destination.

Arles embraces modern artistic expression through its thriving street art and local galleries. Neighborhoods like La Roquette come alive with colorful murals, while independent galleries offer spaces for regional and contemporary artists. The city's cultural calendar is equally dynamic, featuring events like the Les Rencontres d'Arles photography festival and the lively Féria d'Arles. These annual celebrations, blending art, music, and tradition, cement Arles' reputation as a city that continually reinvents itself while honoring its artistic and cultural legacy.

Van Gogh's Legacy in Arles

Vincent van Gogh arrived in Arles in February 1888, seeking the vibrant colors and serene landscapes of the South of France. During his 15-month stay, the city became his muse, inspiring more than 300 works, including some of his most celebrated pieces like Starry Night Over the Rhône, The Yellow House, and Sunflowers. Arles played a transformative role in Van Gogh's artistic development, providing the light and landscapes that helped define his unique style.

Iconic Locations in Van Gogh's Art
Arles' streets, cafes, and surrounding countryside often feature in Van Gogh's paintings. Visitors can explore these places through the Van Gogh Walking Tour, which takes them to landmarks like the Place du Forum (Café Terrace at Night), the Langlois Bridge (The Bridge at Arles), and the Trinquetaille district. While the Yellow House no longer exists, the site is marked for its historical significance.

Fondation Vincent van Gogh
Arles honors Van Gogh's legacy through the Fondation Vincent van Gogh, a cultural institution dedicated to showcasing contemporary art inspired by his work. Although Van Gogh's original paintings are housed elsewhere, the foundation exhibits works by modern artists influenced by his style and vision. It bridges the past and present, continuing Van Gogh's impact on global art.

Museums to Visit

Arles is home to an impressive array of museums, each offering unique insights into the city's artistic, historical, and cultural identity.

Musée Réattu
Housed in a 15th-century Grand Priory of the Order of Malta, the Musée Réattu is a must-visit for art lovers. It showcases works by local artist Jacques Réattu, alongside collections of contemporary art and photography. Notably, the museum features pieces by Pablo Picasso, who donated several drawings to the museum. The building itself, with its stunning riverside location, adds to the charm of this cultural treasure.

Musée de l'Arles Antique
For those fascinated by the city's Roman past, the Musée de l'Arles Antique (Museum of Ancient Arles) is indispensable. The museum houses a remarkable collection of artifacts, including mosaics, sculptures, and everyday items from Roman Arles. Its standout exhibit is the Arles Rhône 3, a well-preserved Roman barge discovered in the Rhône River. Interactive exhibits and detailed reconstructions make this museum both educational and engaging for visitors of all ages.

Other Notable Museums
Arles also boasts smaller but equally captivating institutions, such as the Museon Arlaten, which explores the regional culture and traditions of Provence, and the

Actes Sud Art Center, a hub for modern art and literature. These museums offer a diverse range of experiences, catering to history buffs, art enthusiasts, and casual visitors alike.

Street Art and Local Galleries

While Arles is steeped in history, it also embraces contemporary art forms like street art. The city's walls come alive with murals and graffiti, particularly in the Trinquetaille and La Roquette neighborhoods. These vibrant artworks range from bold political statements to abstract designs, reflecting the dynamic urban culture of Arles.

Local Art Galleries
Arles boasts a thriving community of artists and galleries. Independent galleries like Galerie Huit and L'Espace Van Gogh showcase a mix of traditional and contemporary art, often spotlighting regional talent. These spaces allow visitors to experience the evolving art scene in Provence while discovering up-and-coming artists.

The Role of Photography
Arles is also synonymous with photography, thanks to its renowned Les Rencontres d'Arles festival. Throughout the year, galleries and open-air exhibitions highlight photographic works that challenge and expand the boundaries of visual storytelling. This emphasis on

photography has cemented Arles' status as a hub for modern creative expression.

Annual Cultural Events and Festivals

Arles is a city that knows how to celebrate its cultural identity, with a calendar filled with festivals and events that draw visitors from around the globe.

Les Rencontres d'Arles
This annual photography festival, established in 1970, is Arles' most famous cultural event. Spanning July to September, it transforms the city into an open-air gallery, with exhibitions held in historic venues such as churches, industrial spaces, and Roman ruins. Les Rencontres d'Arles attracts top photographers and artists from around the world, offering workshops, lectures, and thought-provoking installations.

The Féria d'Arles
Twice a year, Arles hosts the Féria, a vibrant festival celebrating the city's bullfighting traditions. Held during Easter and in September, the Féria includes bullfights in the Roman Amphitheatre, parades, live music, and street parties. It's a unique blend of Roman heritage and Provençal culture that captures the city's lively spirit.

Provençal Festivals
Arles also honors its regional heritage through festivals like the Fête des Gardians in May, celebrating the Camargue cowboys and their traditions. Another highlight is the Drôles de Noëls, a magical Christmas

festival featuring performances, markets, and decorations that transform Arles into a winter wonderland.

Contemporary Art and Film Festivals
Beyond traditional celebrations, Arles hosts contemporary events like the Arles Film Festival, which showcases independent films and documentaries, and Les Suds à Arles, a world music festival featuring performances by artists from diverse cultures. These events emphasize Arles' role as a global cultural crossroads.

CHAPTER 6

Culinary Delights of Arles

Arles is a haven for culinary enthusiasts seeking authentic flavors and vibrant local traditions. The city's gastronomy is deeply rooted in Provençal heritage, showcasing a rich tapestry of dishes that highlight fresh, seasonal ingredients like olives, herbs, seafood, and vegetables. From traditional specialties such as La Gardianne de Taureau (a bull meat stew) to creamy Brandade de Morue (salt cod), the cuisine reflects the simplicity and boldness of Mediterranean flavors. Complementing these dishes are the region's renowned wines, particularly its crisp rosés and aromatic reds, which pair perfectly with the flavors of Arles. The city's culinary charm extends beyond its recipes to bustling markets and family-run eateries, where the spirit of Provence comes alive.

In Arles, food is more than sustenance—it's a cultural experience. Rustic bistros, fine dining establishments, and cozy cafés offer a variety of culinary adventures, from hearty traditional meals to innovative takes on classic Provençal recipes. The city's open-air markets, like the Saturday Market on Boulevard des Lices, provide an immersive introduction to local produce, artisanal cheeses, and the finest Camargue rice. For an even deeper exploration, food tours guide visitors through Arles' culinary landscape, combining tastings with cultural insights into its vibrant traditions.

Traditional Provençal Cuisine

The cuisine of Arles reflects the essence of Provençal gastronomy, characterized by its reliance on fresh, seasonal ingredients and Mediterranean influences. The local food tradition emphasizes simplicity, allowing the natural flavors of herbs, olive oil, vegetables, and seafood to shine. Staples like thyme, rosemary, and basil infused dishes with distinctive aromas, while ingredients like garlic, tomatoes, and olives create a symphony of taste.

Signature Dishes of Arles
La Gardianne de Taureau: This iconic dish is a slow-cooked stew made from bull meat, a specialty from the nearby Camargue region. Marinated in red wine and infused with herbs, it reflects the rustic charm of Provençal cooking.

Brandade de Morue: A creamy blend of **salt cod**, olive oil, and garlic, this dish epitomizes the simplicity and bold flavors of the region.

Bouillabaisse: While more commonly associated with Marseille, this rich fish stew is also popular in Arles. Made with fresh local seafood, saffron, and Provençal spices, it's a must-try for visitors.

Tapenade: This classic Provençal spread, made from crushed olives, capers, and anchovies, is a favorite starter, often served with fresh bread.

Camargue Influences
Being close to the Camargue, Arles' cuisine incorporates ingredients unique to this wetland area, such as Camargue rice (a staple used in risottos and salads), sea salt, and beef from the region's distinctive bulls. This connection to the Camargue enriches the culinary diversity of Arles and sets it apart within Provence.

Best Local Restaurants

Arles is home to a variety of fine dining establishments where chefs elevate Provençal flavors with contemporary techniques.

L'Atelier de Jean-Luc Rabanel: This two-Michelin-star restaurant offers a masterful tasting menu celebrating organic, plant-based cuisine inspired by Provençal traditions. Chef Jean-Luc Rabanel's innovative approach has made it a top destination for food connoisseurs.

Le Cilantro: Known for its creative French-Mediterranean fusion, Le Cilantro uses seasonal ingredients to craft dishes that are both sophisticated and deeply rooted in local flavors.

Charming Bistros and Family-Run Eateries**
For a more casual yet equally authentic experience, Arles boasts a variety of bistros and family-run establishments.

Le Criquet: A cozy spot offering traditional Provençal fare, including perfectly cooked seafood dishes like grilled sardines and bouillabaisse.

Le Gibolin: Known for its warm atmosphere and outstanding wine list, this restaurant serves hearty, flavor-packed dishes that celebrate the best of local produce.

Cafés and Snacks
For lighter meals or snacks, Arles' cafés are ideal for enjoying socca (a chickpea pancake), pissaladière (onion tart), or a glass of chilled rosé paired with olives. The Place du Forum, a historic square, is lined with atmospheric cafés perfect for people-watching while sampling these treats.

Regional Wines and Markets

Provence is famous for its wines, particularly its crisp and refreshing rosés. The vineyards surrounding Arles produce exceptional varieties, thanks to the region's sunny climate and unique terroir.

Rosé Wines: These wines are light, aromatic, and perfect for pairing with the region's seafood and vegetable dishes.

Red Wines: Rich and earthy, reds from nearby Les Baux-de-Provence often accompany heartier dishes like La Gardianne de Taureau.

White Wines: Offering floral and citrusy notes, Provençal whites complement the region's fish and vegetarian dishes beautifully.

Exploring the Markets of Arles
Arles' open-air markets are a feast for the senses, showcasing the finest local ingredients.

Saturday Market: Held on Boulevard des Lices, this is one of the largest markets in Provence. Visitors can browse an array of fresh fruits, vegetables, cheeses, cured meats, and baked goods while enjoying the lively atmosphere.

Camargue Salt and Rice: Markets in Arles often feature gourmet salt varieties from the Camargue, along with the region's iconic red and black rice.

Local Specialties: Don't miss trying the region's cheeses, like tomme infused with herbs, or locally produced olive oils and tapenades.

Food Souvenirs
The markets also offer plenty of opportunities to bring a piece of Arles home, with jars of lavender honey, artisanal jams, and Provençal herbs making excellent souvenirs.

Tips for Food Tours

Arles is best explored through a guided food tour that takes visitors on a journey through the city's culinary history. These tours often include visits to the markets, tastings at local eateries, and wine pairings at nearby vineyards.

Hire a Local Guide: Opting for a knowledgeable guide ensures a deeper understanding of Arles' culinary traditions and hidden gems.

Combine History and Food: Many tours integrate visits to historic sites like the Roman Amphitheatre or the Alyscamps Necropolis, enriching the overall experience.

Self-Guided Food Explorations
For independent travelers, a self-guided food tour offers flexibility and discovery.

Start at the Markets: Begin your day by exploring the vibrant markets to pick up local snacks and learn about seasonal ingredients.

Visit the Camargue: Extend your tour with a trip to the Camargue for a hands-on experience, such as visiting rice farms or salt marshes.

Sample Local Specialties: Stop at cafés, bistros, and wine shops to sample regional delicacies.

Seasonal Considerations

Provence's culinary offerings are highly seasonal, so plan your visit to coincide with the availability of specific ingredients or festivals. Spring and summer are ideal for fresh vegetables and seafood, while autumn brings an abundance of mushrooms, truffles, and hearty stews

CHAPTER 7

Natural Escapes and Outdoor Activities

Arles, surrounded by breathtaking landscapes and rich ecosystems, is an ideal destination for outdoor enthusiasts looking to immerse themselves in nature. The nearby **Camargue region**, one of Europe's largest river deltas, offers a unique wetland environment filled with salt flats, lagoons, and lush marshlands. Visitors can explore this stunning area on horseback, by bike, or on guided tours, encountering its famed pink flamingos, wild horses, and black bulls. Alongside the Camargue, the **Rhône River** provides a serene setting for scenic walks, boat cruises, and kayaking, allowing visitors to appreciate both the natural beauty and historical significance of the area.

Arles boasts a variety of hiking and cycling trails that traverse the Provençal countryside, offering panoramic views of vineyards, olive groves, and limestone hills. Trails like the ViaRhôna and those within the Alpilles Regional Park cater to adventurers of all skill levels. Additionally, the region is a haven for birdwatchers and wildlife lovers, with over 400 species of birds and diverse fauna inhabiting its landscapes. Whether exploring the wetlands, strolling along the riverbanks, or engaging in outdoor sports, Arles provides a perfect balance of tranquility, adventure, and ecological discovery.

Exploring the Camargue Region

The Camargue is a vast and stunning wetland area located to the south of Arles, nestled between the Mediterranean Sea and the Rhône River delta. Covering over 930 square kilometers, it is one of Europe's largest river deltas and is celebrated for its unique ecosystems. Its combination of marshes, salt flats, lagoons, and meadows creates a haven for flora and fauna.

Key Attractions in the Camargue
The Camargue Natural Regional Park: This protected area offers numerous trails and observation points, making it an ideal destination for nature lovers. Visitors can explore the vast salt flats, encounter wild horses, and marvel at the region's diverse vegetation.

The Pink Salt Flats of Salin-de-Giraud: These striking pink-hued salt pans are a must-see for their ethereal beauty and historical significance in salt production.

Saintes-Maries-de-la-Mer: This charming seaside town serves as the gateway to the Camargue, offering beaches, cultural sites, and opportunities to experience the region's traditions.

Outdoor Activities in the Camargue
Visitors to the Camargue can partake in a variety of activities, including horseback riding on the region's iconic Camargue horses, cycling through scenic trails, and guided tours by 4x4 or boat to explore its most

remote corners. These activities allow for an immersive experience of the wetlands' serene beauty.

Rhône River Walks and Activities

The Rhône River, which flows through Arles, has played a vital role in shaping the city's history, culture, and natural environment. Today, it provides a picturesque backdrop for outdoor activities and leisurely exploration.

Walking Along the RhônePromenade Along the Riverbanks: The riverbanks of the Rhône offer serene walking paths where visitors can enjoy views of the water, historic landmarks, and lush vegetation. Strolling along these paths at sunrise or sunset is a particularly enchanting experience.

Historical Highlights: Walks along the Rhône often lead to key sites like the Roman Bridge of Arles and remnants of ancient river infrastructure that speak to its historical importance.

Activities on the Rhône
Boat Cruises: Guided boat tours on the Rhône River are a popular way to explore the region from a different perspective. These cruises often include commentary on the history and ecology of the area.

Kayaking and Canoeing: For those seeking a more active experience, kayaking and canoeing along the Rhône provide a unique opportunity to connect with its natural beauty while enjoying some light exercise.

Fishing: The Rhône is home to a variety of fish species, making it a favorite spot for recreational anglers.

Hiking and Cycling Routes

Arles is surrounded by picturesque landscapes, offering numerous hiking opportunities for all levels of experience.

The Alpilles Regional Park: Located just a short drive from Arles, the Alpilles offer trails that wind through rugged limestone hills, olive groves, and vineyards. Hikers can enjoy breathtaking views of Provence while exploring this tranquil area.

The Camargue Trails: The flat terrain of the Camargue makes it ideal for leisurely hikes. Trails often lead through marshlands, salt flats, and bird habitats, allowing for close encounters with the region's wildlife.

Cycling Routes Around Arles
Cycling is one of the best ways to explore the scenic landscapes of Arles and its surroundings.

The ViaRhôna: This long-distance cycling route connects Lake Geneva to the Mediterranean, passing through Arles along the way. Cyclists can enjoy views of the Rhône River and the Provençal countryside.

The Camargue Cycling Paths: The Camargue features flat and well-maintained cycling routes that lead to highlights like the pink salt flats and Saintes-Maries-de-la-Mer.

Alpilles Routes: For more adventurous cyclists, the Alpilles offer challenging routes with rewarding views of vineyards and ancient villages.

Tips for Hikers and Cyclists
Stay Hydrated: The Provençal sun can be intense, especially in summer. Always carry water.

Plan for Wildlife Encounters: Many trails pass through areas inhabited by birds, bulls, and horses. Maintain a respectful distance to avoid disturbing the animals.

Use Local Maps: Obtain maps from local tourist offices to ensure you follow marked trails and avoid getting lost.

Birdwatching and Wildlife Experiences

The Camargue is one of Europe's premier destinations for birdwatching, with over 400 bird species calling the region home.

Flamingos: The Camargue is renowned for its flocks of pink flamingos, which thrive in its saltwater lagoons. The Pont de Gau Ornithological Park is a particularly good spot to observe these majestic birds up close.

Herons and Egrets: Along with flamingos, the wetlands are filled with herons, egrets, and other wading birds.

Migratory Birds: The Camargue serves as an important stopover for migratory birds, offering opportunities to see rare species depending on the season.

Wildlife Beyond Birds
While birdwatching is a highlight, the Camargue is also home to a variety of other wildlife.

Camargue Horses: These semi-wild white horses are iconic symbols of the region. They can often be seen grazing in marshes or carrying riders through the countryside.

Black Bulls: The region's bulls are raised for traditional bullfighting events and are integral to the culture of the Camargue.

Fish and Amphibians: The wetlands support diverse aquatic life, including fish, frogs, and turtles.

Wildlife Tours and Safaris
Visitors can join guided tours led by naturalists to learn more about the region's ecology and wildlife. These tours often include bird watching excursions, visits to horse and bull farms, and insights into the delicate balance of the Camargue ecosystem.

CHAPTER 8

Shopping in Arles

Shopping in Arles is a delightful blend of tradition and modernity, reflecting the city's rich cultural heritage and vibrant local economy. Traditional Provençal markets, such as the renowned Arles Market, offer a sensory feast with stalls brimming with fresh produce, regional delicacies, and handcrafted goods. These markets not only provide visitors with an authentic taste of Provençal life but also serve as social hubs where locals and tourists mingle. Beyond the markets, artisan boutiques showcase the city's craftsmanship, offering unique souvenirs like pottery, textiles, jewelry, and lavender-based products that capture the essence of Provence.

Arles caters to modern tastes with its shopping centers, high-street stores, and designer boutiques. These venues offer a range of contemporary products, from fashion to electronics, alongside concept stores that merge art, design, and Provençal flair. Local specialties such as olive oil, gourmet tapenades, and regional wines highlight the city's culinary heritage, making them perfect mementos or gifts.

Traditional Provençal Markets

The Provençal markets in Arles are quintessential to its culture and provide a sensory feast for visitors. These markets are not just places to shop but vibrant social hubs where locals and tourists mingle while enjoying the region's finest products.

The Arles Market
The Arles Market, held every Wednesday and Saturday, is among the largest and most renowned in Provence. It stretches over two kilometers, offering a mix of food, crafts, clothing, and household goods. Stalls brim with colorful fruits, vegetables, cheeses, spices, and fresh herbs, capturing the essence of Mediterranean cuisine. Local specialties such as tapenade, saucissons (sausages), and bread make the market a foodie's paradise.

Specialty Markets
Antique Market: Arles is also known for its antique and flea markets. Held periodically, these markets attract collectors and enthusiasts searching for vintage treasures, including furniture, ceramics, and textiles.

Seasonal Markets: During festive seasons, such as Christmas, special markets feature handcrafted ornaments, Provençal nativity figurines (santons), and artisanal food products.

Tips for Visiting Markets
Visiting Provençal markets can be overwhelming due to their size and variety. Arrive early to beat the crowds, wear comfortable shoes, and bring cash as many vendors do not accept cards.

Artisan Boutiques and Souvenirs

Arles is a hub for artisans who craft unique products inspired by the region's culture and natural beauty. The city's boutiques offer one-of-a-kind souvenirs that make for meaningful mementos or gifts.

Handcrafted Pottery and Ceramics
Provençal pottery is a popular item in Arles. Local artisans create vibrant ceramics, including plates, bowls, and decorative pieces adorned with traditional motifs like olives and lavender. These handmade items are available in small workshops and boutiques across the city.

Textiles and Provençal Fabrics
Fabrics from Provence, known for their bright patterns and high quality, are widely sold in Arles. Shops offer tablecloths, napkins, and curtains featuring traditional designs such as floral and paisley prints. These textiles are perfect for adding a touch of Provence to your home.

Jewelry and Accessories
Boutiques in Arles feature jewelry made by local designers, often incorporating materials like leather, silver, and semi-precious stones. Accessories inspired by the region's Roman and medieval history are also popular, reflecting the city's artistic spirit.

Traditional Provençal Souvenirs
From lavender sachets to hand-painted santons, visitors can find a variety of traditional souvenirs. Other popular

items include olive-wood utensils, handcrafted soaps, and artisanal perfumes made from local ingredients.

Local Products: Lavender, Olive Oil, and More

Arles is celebrated for its high-quality local products, which embody the flavors, scents, and artistry of Provence. Purchasing these items not only supports the local economy but also provides an authentic taste of the region.

Lavender Products*
Lavender, the iconic symbol of Provence, is a must-buy in Arles. Shops and markets sell a range of lavender-based products, including:

Essential Oils: Known for their calming properties, lavender oils are widely used in aromatherapy.

Soaps and Candles: Infused with the soothing scent of lavender, these products make wonderful gifts.

Dried Lavender Sachets: These sachets are perfect for scenting drawers or as decorative accents.

Olive Oil and Gourmet Products
Provençal olive oil is highly regarded for its flavor and quality. In Arles, visitors can purchase artisanal olive oils directly from producers or specialty shops. Other gourmet items include:

Tapenades: Olive-based spreads flavored with herbs and garlic.

Herbes de Provence: A fragrant mix of dried herbs used in Mediterranean cooking.

Honey and Jams: Often made with local ingredients like lavender or figs.

Wines and Spirits
Arles is located near some of Providence's finest vineyards, making it an excellent place to shop for regional wines. Visitors can find rosés, reds, and whites, as well as spirits like pastis, a traditional anise-flavored aperitif.

Artisanal Beauty Products
The Provence region is known for its beauty products made from natural ingredients. Arles offers a variety of artisanal soaps, lotions, and perfumes crafted from lavender, olive oil, and other local resources.

Modern Shopping Venues

While Arles is best known for its traditional and artisanal shopping, the city also boasts modern retail options, ensuring that visitors can find everything they need.

Shopping Centers and Malls
Arles features shopping centers with a mix of international brands and local retailers. These venues

are ideal for those seeking convenience and a wide selection of products in one location.

High-Street Shopping
The city center is home to a variety of shops, ranging from fashion boutiques to electronics stores. Popular streets like Rue de la République are lined with stores offering both contemporary and classic styles.

Designer and Concept Stores
For unique and stylish finds, Arles has several concept stores that blend art, fashion, and design. These stores cater to modern tastes while often incorporating elements of Provençal culture.

Bookstores and Art Shops
Given Arles' connection to art and photography, the city has several excellent bookstores and art supply shops. These venues are perfect for finding books on Provençal culture or materials for creative projects.

Supermarkets and Everyday Needs
For practical shopping, Arles has supermarkets and general stores offering groceries, household items, and other essentials. These stores are conveniently located throughout the city.

CHAPTER 9

Accommodation Options

Arles offers a wide array of accommodation options that cater to diverse preferences and budgets. Luxury hotels and boutique resorts provide premium comfort and world-class amenities, ideal for those seeking indulgence and relaxation. For budget-conscious travelers, the city offers affordable choices such as budget hotels, hostels, and vacation rentals, ensuring a comfortable stay without breaking the bank. Visitors can also immerse themselves in the region's charm by staying in unique lodgings like historic inns and traditional Provençal farmhouses, which provide a blend of cultural authenticity and modern comforts.

When planning a stay in Arles, location and personal preferences play an important role in choosing the ideal accommodation. Whether opting for the convenience of city-center hotels, the tranquility of countryside retreats, or the personalized service of boutique lodgings, travelers are guaranteed a memorable experience. Practical tips, such as booking early, reading reviews, and prioritizing amenities, ensure a seamless and enjoyable stay in this captivating Provençal destination.

Luxury Hotels and Resorts

For travelers seeking premium comfort and indulgence, Arles boasts a range of luxury hotels and resorts that provide world-class amenities and exceptional service.

Five-Star Hotels

Arles is home to a handful of five-star properties that combine opulent interiors with Provençal charm. These hotels often feature spacious rooms and suites, fine dining restaurants, and spa facilities, making them perfect for a lavish getaway. Many of these establishments are located in historic buildings, offering a blend of elegance and cultural authenticity.

Boutique Hotel

Boutique hotels in Arles provide a more intimate and personalized luxury experience. These smaller properties are often independently owned and feature unique design elements inspired by the local heritage. Many boutique hotels are located in the city center, within walking distance of major attractions like the Roman amphitheater and the Van Gogh Foundation.

Resort-Style Stays

Just outside Arles, luxury resorts offer a tranquil retreat amidst the region's natural beauty. Surrounded by lavender fields or olive groves, these properties provide amenities such as infinity pools, wellness centers, and gourmet dining experiences. Resorts are ideal for those looking to combine relaxation with exploration.

Benefits of Luxury Stays

Luxury accommodations in Arles provide personalized services such as concierge assistance, private tours, and curated experiences, ensuring guests have a memorable stay. These establishments are also perfect for special occasions like honeymoons or anniversaries.

Budget-Friendly Stays

Arles caters to budget-conscious travelers with an array of affordable accommodations that do not compromise on comfort or quality.

Budget Hotels
Several budget hotel chains operate in and around Arles, offering clean and comfortable rooms at reasonable prices. These hotels typically provide basic amenities, such as Wi-Fi, air conditioning, and breakfast options, making them ideal for travelers prioritizing value.

Hostels and Guesthouses
Hostels in Arles are a popular choice for backpackers and solo travelers. These establishments offer shared dormitories, private rooms, and communal spaces where guests can connect with fellow travelers. Guesthouses, on the other hand, provide a more homely atmosphere, often run by local families who offer insights into the city's culture.

Vacation Rentals
For those looking to save money while enjoying the comforts of home, vacation rentals are an excellent option. Platforms like Airbnb and Vrbo offer a wide range of apartments, studios, and small houses in Arles. These accommodations are particularly suitable for longer stays, families, or groups.

Tips for Budget Travel

To secure the best deals on budget accommodations, book well in advance, especially during peak tourist seasons. Additionally, consider staying slightly outside the city center, where prices are often lower, and public transportation provides easy access to attractions.

Unique Stays: Historic Inns and Farmhouses

For a truly memorable experience, Arles offers unique lodging options that reflect the region's history and rural charm.

Historic Inns

Staying in a historic inn allows guests to immerse themselves in the city's rich past. Many of these inns are located in centuries-old buildings that have been carefully restored to preserve their architectural features while incorporating modern comforts. These properties often exude a romantic ambiance, making them ideal for couples.

Traditional Farmhouses (Mas)

Outside the city, Provençal farmhouses, known as "mas," provide a rustic and serene escape. These traditional stone buildings are surrounded by vineyards, olive groves, or sunflower fields, offering a quintessential Provençal experience. Many farmhouses have been converted into charming bed-and-breakfasts or boutique lodgings. Guests can enjoy activities such as farm-to-table dining, wine tasting, and countryside walks.

Unique Features of Historic and Rural Stays
Cultural Immersion: These accommodations often reflect the local heritage through their architecture, décor, and hospitality.

Personalized Service: Smaller establishments provide personalized attention, with hosts often sharing stories about the property's history.

Peaceful Atmosphere: Farmhouses and historic inns are ideal for those seeking a quiet and relaxing environment away from the bustling city center.

Booking Tips
These unique accommodations are often limited in availability, so early booking is essential, particularly during the summer months. Look for properties with good reviews and consider contacting hosts directly for specific requests or recommendations.

Tips for Booking the Perfect Accommodation

Choosing the right place to stay in Arles requires careful consideration of several factors, including budget, location, and personal preferences.

Determine Your Priorities
Before booking, decide on the key features you value most in your accommodation. Are you looking for proximity to attractions, luxurious amenities, or a unique cultural experience? Clarifying your priorities will help narrow down your options.

Consider the Location
City Center: Staying in the city center provides easy access to Arles' main attractions, such as the Roman monuments and museums.

Countryside: Opt for rural accommodations if you prefer a tranquil environment and wish to explore the natural beauty of Provence.

Transportation: Check the availability of public transport or parking if you plan to stay outside the city center.

Read Reviews and Ratings
Online reviews and ratings from previous guests provide valuable insights into the quality and service of accommodations. Pay attention to comments about cleanliness, customer service, and the accuracy of property descriptions.

Compare Prices
Use booking platforms to compare prices across different accommodations. Look for deals or discounts, especially during the off-season, and consider booking

directly through the property's website for potential perks or savings.

Check Amenities and Policies
Ensure that the accommodation offers the amenities you require, such as Wi-Fi, air conditioning, or breakfast. Familiarize yourself with cancellation policies to avoid unexpected charges in case of changes to your travel plans.

Book Early
Arles is a popular tourist destination, especially during events like the Rencontres d'Arles photography festival. Booking early ensures better availability and competitive prices, particularly for unique or luxury stays.

CHAPTER 10

Planning Your Itinerary

Planning your itinerary for a trip to Arles is essential to fully experience the city's rich cultural and historical offerings. With its Roman ruins, charming old town, and Provençal ambiance, Arles offers visitors a variety of attractions and activities. Whether you have one day, a weekend, or a few days to explore, crafting a thoughtful plan ensures that you can immerse yourself in its unique heritage. Suggested itineraries include visits to iconic landmarks like the Arles Amphitheater and Van Gogh sites, day trips to nearby towns, and adventures in the natural beauty of the Camargue.

Practical advice on packing and preparation can enhance your trip. Essential tips include choosing the best time to visit, understanding transportation options, and booking accommodations early. Packing comfortable shoes, lightweight clothing, and sun protection is important for exploring the city and countryside.

Suggested 1-Day Itinerary

If you have only one day to explore Arles, focus on the city's most iconic landmarks and cultural highlights. This itinerary is perfect for those on a short visit or a day trip.

Morning: Roman Heritage
Start at the Arles Amphitheater (Arènes d'Arles):** Visit the city's most famous Roman landmark, a well-preserved amphitheater that once hosted gladiatorial games. Explore its history and take in stunning views from the top.

Visit the Roman Theater: Just a short walk away, this ancient theater is another testament to Arles' Roman history, where performances still take place today.

Midday: Van Gogh's Footsteps
Lunch in Place du Forum: Enjoy a meal at one of the cafes or restaurants in this lively square, which inspired Vincent van Gogh's painting Café Terrace at Night.

Walk to the Van Gogh Trail: Explore sites associated with Van Gogh's life in Arles, such as the Espace Van Gogh and the spot where he painted The Starry Night Over the Rhône.

Afternoon: Museums and Art
Visit the Fondation Vincent van Gogh: This modern art museum celebrates the legacy of Van Gogh and often features rotating exhibitions.

Explore the Arles Museum of Antiquity: Learn about Arles' Roman past through its extensive collection of artifacts, mosaics, and sculptures.

Evening: Sunset at the Rhône
End your day by taking a leisurely stroll along the Rhône River. Capture the serene beauty of the sunset as it reflects on the water—a view that inspired many artists.

Suggested 3-Day Itinerary

A three-day visit allows for a more in-depth exploration of Arles and its surrounding areas, combining history, art, and Provençal charm.

Day 1: Explore Arles
Follow the 1-day itinerary above to explore Arles' Roman ruins, Van Gogh's landmarks, and museums. Spend your first day soaking in the city's highlights.

Day 2: Beyond the City
Morning: Visit the Camargue: Take a short trip to the Camargue Natural Regional Park, known for its wild horses, flamingos, and salt marshes. Enjoy birdwatching or a guided horse-riding tour to experience the region's unique biodiversity.

Lunch in Saintes-Maries-de-la-Mer: Visit this picturesque seaside town in the Camargue, known for its sandy beaches and charming atmosphere.

Afternoon: Return to Arles for Art Exploration: Visit the LUMA Arles arts complex, a cutting-edge cultural center that houses modern art exhibits and installations.

Day 3: Day Trip to Nearby Towns
Morning: Discover Les Baux-de-Provence: Explore this medieval hilltop village and visit attractions such as the Château des Baux and the immersive Carrières de Lumières art exhibition.

Afternoon: Stroll Through Saint-Rémy-de-Provence: Famous for its connection to Van Gogh, this quaint town offers shops, cafes, and Roman ruins, such as the Glanum archaeological site.

Evening: Return to Arles: Conclude your trip with a relaxed dinner in one of Arles' traditional Provençal restaurants.

Weekend Getaway Ideas

For those planning a weekend getaway in Arles, here are a few curated ideas based on different interests.

History and Culture Weekend
Day 1: Visit the Roman Amphitheater, the Roman Theater, and the Arles Museum of Antiquity. Take a walking tour of the historic center, including the Church of St. Trophime.

Day 2: Explore the Van Gogh Trail and the Fondation Vincent van Gogh. Spend the afternoon at LUMA Arles, followed by a sunset walk along the Rhône River.

Nature and Adventure Weekend
Day 1:Start with a morning trip to the Camargue, enjoying activities like birdwatching or horseback riding. In the evening, return to Arles for dinner.

Day 2: Take a day trip to Les Baux-de-Provence or the Alpilles Natural Regional Park, where you can hike and enjoy the stunning landscapes of Provence.

Art and Photography Weekend
Day 1: Visit the Fondation Vincent van Gogh and the LUMA Arles complex. Explore the Espace Van Gogh for inspiration.

Day 2: Take a photography tour of the Camargue or Les Baux-de-Provence, capturing the scenic beauty of the region.

Travel Tips and Packing Checklist

Travel Tips
Arles is most enjoyable in spring (April to June) and fall (September to October) when the weather is mild, and crowds are smaller.

Summers can be hot and busy, especially during the Rencontres d'Arles photography festival.

Transportation
Arles is pedestrian-friendly, with most attractions within walking distance.

Use regional trains or buses to explore nearby towns and the Camargue. Renting a car is recommended for more flexibility in rural areas.

Dining Recommendations
Try traditional Provençal dishes like ratatouille, bouillabaisse, and tapenade.

Visit local markets to sample fresh produce and regional specialties.

Booking Tips
Reserve accommodations and tickets for popular attractions in advance, especially during peak seasons.

Look for combination tickets to save money when visiting multiple museums or historical sites.

Clothing and Accessories
Comfortable walking shoes for exploring cobblestone streets and archaeological sites.

Lightweight clothing for warm days and layers for cooler evenings.

A wide-brimmed hat, sunglasses, and sunscreen to protect against the Provençal sun.

Travel Essentials
A reusable water bottle to stay hydrated while exploring.

A guidebook or map of Arles and the surrounding areas.

A power adapter for European outlets if needed.

Photography and Art Supplies
A camera or smartphone for capturing the picturesque streets and landscapes.

Sketchbooks or notebooks for artists inspired by Arles' scenery and culture.

Miscellaneous
Binoculars for birdwatching in the Camargue.

A small backpack or tote bag for carrying essentials during day trips.

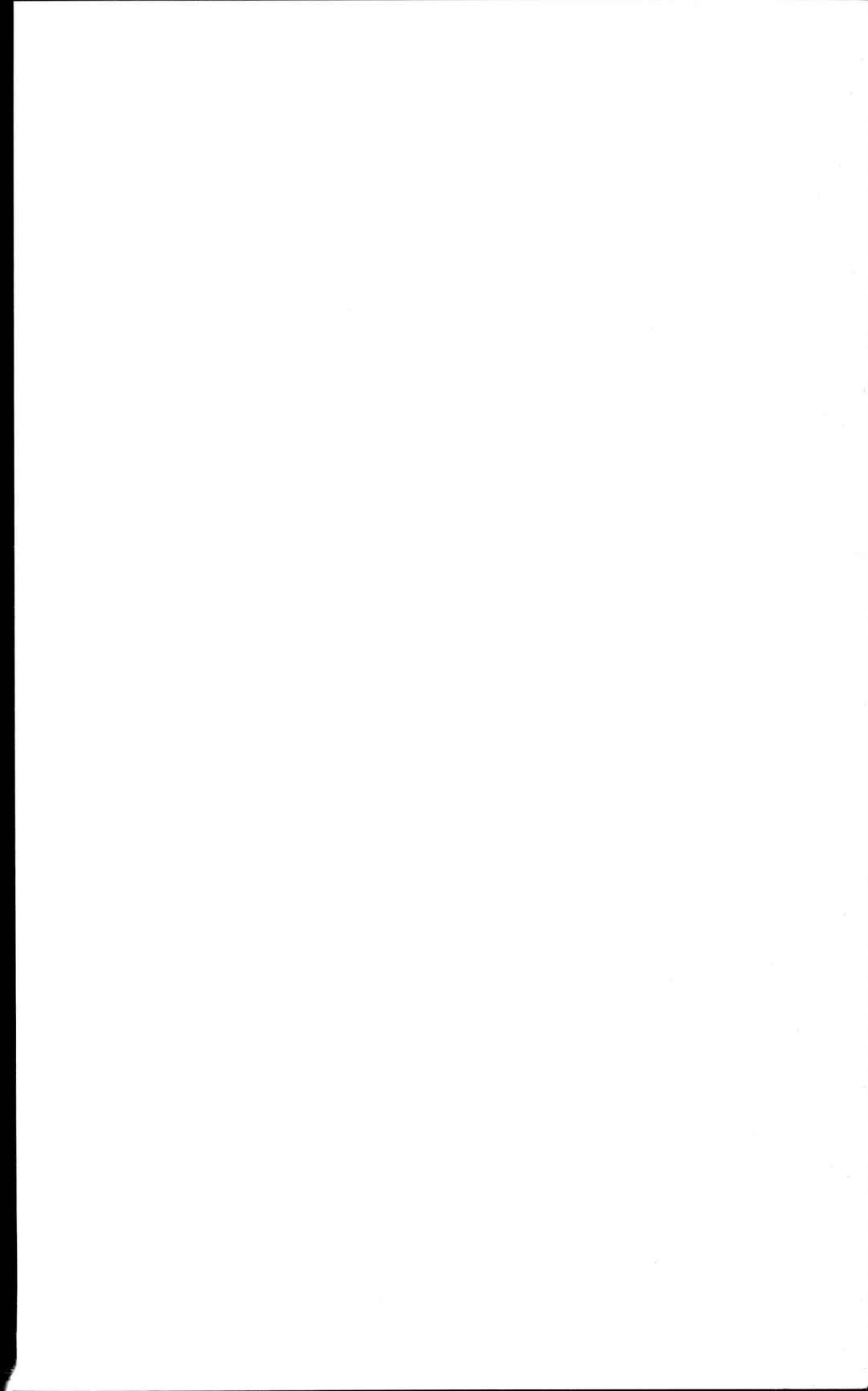

Printed in Great Britain
by Amazon